SENSE OF SOLACE

MARK JACK

INDIA • SINGAPORE • MALAYSIA

ISBN 979-8-89632-352-5

A Note of Gratitude for Nature and the Universe

Gratitude fills my thoughts as I observe the balance of nature and the grandeur of the cosmos. The sun illuminates our days, the moon brings calm to our nights, and the stars inspire us with their eternal brilliance. Each planet, with its quiet orbit, enhances the harmony of the vast expanse.

The rivers shape paths through landscapes, the winds carry life across the earth, the trees and plants transform sunlight into the air we breathe, and the drops of rain nourish the earth. Each element, from the smallest grain of sand to the largest galaxy, is a testament to the complexity and beauty of existence.

To everything that makes this world vibrant and alive, I offer my thanks - not to a being , but to the phenomena that sustain and inspire us.

With gratitude for the existence itself,

Mark Jack

Hand- Drawn Illustrations

Anjaly Babu & Naslin Rasheed

Neha Thomas, the Publishing Manager; Akshaya J., the Publishing Consultant; and the crew at Notion Press Publishing for their unwavering support and expertise in bringing this book to fruition.

Contents

Priceless

I left so much time slip away;
At times, I never cherished its worth.
Unaware of how swiftly time goes by,
Never anticipated it would circle back.

Time did not occupy my thoughts,
I was never the one to watch the clock closely.
I did not craft moments in the fabric of time;
Drifted like a wandering cloud in the velvet sky.

Time dances and gallops when laughter paints the day;

Time crawls like a tired snail in office hours.

Time flows with its own rhythm, painting life's canvas with moments.

Time's nature is contained within the steady pulse of a clock.

In the cosmic theatre, everything performs,

To the eternal script of time.

Everything is sculpted by time's hand,

Every living soul wears the clock of age,

As a silent badge of honor.

Time refracts the light that envelops our world.

Time unfolds its mysteries uniquely,
For each person it encounters.
Time is truly individual,
And to be truly individual is priceless.

A Constant Light

In my life, there's someone who's there through every turn-

Through shadows and clear skies her presence is constant.

Not just beside me, but as part of who I am.

She's beautiful, not only the way she appears,

But in the quiet strength she brings, the patience,

The way she holds us steady, like roots grounding the tallest tree.

A kind heart person beyond measure.
A forgiver of my mistakes big and small.
And never letting me feel the weight of it,
Nor showing the shadow it may have cast.

I admire her trust, her ability to see the good in us.
At times, my mind may drift, clouded and uncertain.
But in my heart, she holds the primary place.

Since we began this journey together,

We've become something like friends who understand,

Who give each other space, yet never drift apart.

In her, I find freedom, I find calm.

Words can't contain the gratitude,

The silent respect that lives in me for her.

She is my anchor, strength that let me stand firmly

Secured, grounded, emotionally, mentally and financially stable.

The Perimeter Of My Universe

Mornings that never break,
Nights that stay on.
Our dew of sweat that forever remain,
Inseparable moments under a Velvet Sky.

The clock ticks its rhythmic cadence,
Infusing meaning to words that belong only to us.
We entwined as one, with intervals in between,
Realizing together that we were done.

My heart will never let you go;
You will remain within me for eternal.
You are the dawn, you are the dusk,
The core of joy, The perimeter of my universe.

Spider-Man's Mirage: Far From Humans

Even Spider-Man awoke to a bitter truth,
That serving mankind held no worth.
He saw the selfishness humans tried to hide,
And found more truth in the animals' eyes.

In their loyal hearts, in their honest ways,
No lies, no greed, no empty games—
Just pure souls who loved him the same.
In their silence, he found his place,
Far from humanity's cruel, empty chase.

In these centuries, where greed's shadows thrive,
He wonders if goodness still keeps us alive.
He wearies of saving hearts that now pale—
Spider-Man's mirage, a kindness gone stale.

Liquid Gold And Its Miraculous Makers

Golden syrup, sweet and thick,
Nature's gift, a healing trick.
From blossoms kissed by morning's dew,
Comes a treasure pure and true.

Liquid amber, dense and bright,
A soothing elixir, a gentle light,
Crafted by winged workers, small yet grand,
In hexagonal homes, they carefully guard.

A medicine stored in the tiny cells,
Where stories of health and sweetness dwell.
Punctual pollinators in harmonious flight,
Gathering sunlight drops, morning till night.

Nutritional bullets, pure and rare,
Crafted with precision, love, and care.
In every drop, the essence shines,
A timeless gift from ancient times.

So raise a spoon, a toast to pollinators—
Their golden labor, a miracle with ease.
For in each taste, a world unfolds
Of liquid gold, as the story is told—
A tribute to sweet liquid gold and its miraculous makers.

Yet Some Flowers Aren't Meant For Light

The last words of her echoed, soft and clear,
I think my choice was wrong.
Did I assume she was close to me ?
Or Overthink what we were meant to be ?
Her words remained restless in my heart,
In them, a truth I cannot find.
Yet they cut deep like silent emotions,
Awakening all my hidden fears.

Was she close to me, or was I blind?
To feelings I could never bind?
Her parting words still echo long,
A quiet ache, a stolen song.
She never saw a friend in me,
A truth I've now begun to see.
The bond I cherished starts to fade,
As night consumes the light of day.

And now its time to say good bye,
To the Lotus that bloomed in my slum pond.
From mud it bloomed, pure and bright,
Yet some flowers aren't meant for light.

The Hues of Toe Tips

Each touch, each shape, each careful line,
A glimpse of perfection, a hint of style.
But rather, it's a subtle art—
In natural and other hues, nails that speak.

For in those fingers, a tale is spun
Of who they are and what's begun.
Not the face or form so grand,
But the beauty in a woman's hand.

A simple touch of color or clear,
For in the shape and careful trim,
Reveals a woman's care—
Of hygiene and beauty entwined.

It begins with a simple, vivid sight:
A baby pink hue that caught the light.
One of a friend's toes, so gently laid—
My love for nails grows and grows.

Collecting images, a cherished trove,
Of friends' nail art where my heart roves.
A wallpaper bright, a cherished view,
Of manicure hues so true—
The hues of toe tips.

The True Essence Of Life's Hunger

In the tall walls of a great firm, my journey quietly began,

A first spark of ambition, simple hopes, and a humble plan.

The firm was epic, yet the pay was thin,

And surviving grew tougher, day by day.

My commitments were vast, but I stood tall,

Running life's show, steady through it.

One day at work, worn and strained,

With silent worries, I quietly remained.

Sales targets loomed like concrete walls,
Draining me daily, though I tried hard.
Lunchtime came, but what a sight—
An empty lunchbox, just water in sight.

To dodge questions and quietly retreat,
I wandered to a nearby park and found my seat.
Inhaled the fresh, green air and let out a sigh,
As if I'd feasted on a meal piled high.

And there I realized in that simple situation
Poverty is the greatest that's ever been

With nothing to eat and pride in dismay
I learned that wealth isn't just what we bring in.
In the park, I sit quiet, with no meal to eat,
I realized the true essence of life's hunger.

My Heart Does Pine For The Joy Once Felt Fine

On a lively Saturday night,
With friends and laughter,
In the midst of revelry amid the throng,
We danced in rhythm, our spirits high.

Among the chatter and clinking glass,
A chance encounter, a passing moment.
In the pub's warm, vibrant scene,
A stranger's smile felt almost serene.

Amid the crowd, my gaze did land,
On her eyes, and she was looking at me.
A red gown that flowed,
In that moment, nothing else compared.

I pointed my index finger towards her,
To get the attention of my friend.
She saw me, and my hand gesture—
It was a very straight spark.

She was average, still she was beautiful,
But the spark shared was strong and alluring.
Only once I saw her like a dream,
In that pub's soft blue light.

Afterward, I never searched for her there,
A memory lost in the night's sway.

The next day dawned with a hangover.
Scrolling through the social page,
There she was, the same red light.
With a racing heart, I took a chance.

I sent her a follow request, a digital dance.
She accepted and sent one too.
In likes and comments, a story spun.
Thus, we started a bond between us.

After that, messages flowed,
In chats that grew both old and new.
Casual exchanges, day by day,
Updates shared in a friendly style.

A Fleeting Muse

The sea hums with whispers of waves.
As daylight is about to end its dance with clouds,
Painting the sky in rhyme.
A half cup of sipped latte, the day's thoughts held at bay.

Linen soft as second skin,
Pure white drop shoulder shirt,
Nude legs.
A breeze of finesse, though simple in its flirt.

At my 9 o'clock, her presence near,
With bunny-tied hair I see her clear—
Ebony skin, like gold-kissed mud from a volcano's heart,
A sculptor's mark striking sexiness on beauty overgrown.

But as words began to take flight,
And as my pen approached the edge of delight,
Her chariot arrived, whisking her away.
A quick encounter turned to yesterday.
She rose, and with her, my writing drifted—a fleeting muse.

The Stewards
Of Siren's Brew

In Siren's world where time slows its speed,
Thrice or more each passing week I find my space,
There upon the left of Siren's portrait,
Mastrena II hums, brewing espresso essence.

Behind the shining brew, a few faces appear,
Smiles that quill the passing years.
With charm, they summon names in tones so sweet,
When the orders are ready to be collected.

They stand unwavering, bright and confident,
Slim and tall with a radiant smile.
Their hands a guide in silent air,
A gesture speaks as my order takes flight.

A tall 'Americano' or 'Emperor's Clouds & Mist' of green,
From their swift hands serene and keen.
Among them, making choice for best a delightful challenge,
The vibrant Mandarin Fishes in Siren's range.

Oh! They shimmer with glow.

With every visit, their warmth brightly shows.

The joy they spin, the solace they bestow,

Making each visit a moment to mend and glow.

You Will Eternally Be My Cup Of Esteem

In a cup no more than eight ounces,
A drink so rich and dark brown.
Its spirit lingers, cocoa's fragrance,
A marshmallow on top, resting softly.

A hot sip and slurp begins a gentle quaff,
A song of flavors nestled inside.
Sixty percent chocolate, bold and bittersweet,
Forty percent milk—the symmetry complete.

Still, I, a dreamer of bold bitterness,
Wish for ninety percent of cocoa's richness,
A bitter kiss that ignites my taste buds,
A euphoric thrill, a blend that draws me in.

Yet when savored in lukewarm,
Its richness melts my heart's purple wall,
Lush and velvety even as it cools—
A sublime elixir, draped in robust zest.

Oh, S'more Hot Chocolate, my dark delight,
No other drink has triumphed to your summit.
Until a rival shows up in my heart's gaze,
You will eternally be my cup of esteem.

An Ode To A Timeless Hijab Beauty

Across the café, in silence we sat,
On calls, yet more than that.
Diagonally sitting, a world of worlds apart,
But a shared smile sparkled, bridging the space between us.
It was an unspoken signal and an unseen impulse,
Causing my pen to flow with verses,
As if moved by its own harmony.

In a kameez with elegance so rare,
A scarf draped softly with tender care.
Half her head the fabric did veil,
Yet her beauty no cloth could pale.

Framing her face, a few strands stray,
Like the split tail of a "Racket-Tailed Drongo."
Eyebrows arched like a crescent moon;
In black, they danced a rainbow tune.

Her nose petite, with a falcon's flair,
Carved with precision beyond compare.
Her lips so small, in nude hues, lay soft and subtle;
They charm with an open smile.
Finger nails in a gentle hue —
Together, all make her elegance anew.

For she departed too fleetly,

Leaving the reflections tangled and fragmentary.

Overall, it emphasized the lasting and

Profound impact of her enchanting magnetism.

For here, an “Ode to a Timeless Hijab Beauty”

Remains unfinished.

Every Star Leads Back To You

Beneath the velvet sky so clear,
I watch the evening star appear.
In the west, where Venus shines,
Her glow reminds me you're sublime.

A gem of light, soft in its gleam,
Just like you in every dream.
The night's caress, a gentle cue,
That every star leads back to you.

And Here I Stand Waiting

My heart forever longs to send her words,
But my hand pulls away.
I fret that my words might vex her,
Or she might have no words to send my way.

Her name lights up in my chats,
But I leave it unseen,
Trying to seem busy,
Though that's not what I mean.

I hope she does the same,
Though it's just a passing thought—
A little game of absence,
Pretending we're caught.

I wrote her a poem,
Many lines about her beauty,
But every message dances around
When we might meet.

She never rejects, just smiles with a "we'll see,"
Or a hopeful "let's hope so" and "I'd love to."

Still, I wait for her words,
The ones I long to hear:
"I am coming soon, tomorrow or next month."
My eyes just wait.

For she's close by, within my country's line,
But time is slipping—only three months left to find.

And here I stand, waiting
With my black ink letters for her,
Ready to cherish her,
But her plans still not sure.

With Rising Thrill

Tomorrow comes with an arising thrill
To see her again at Café Lady Laofella.
My heart stands excited
Until her gaze is finally near.
I am eager for that eye's sweet mark;
With every glance, the world will sway.
I wait for her as dawn brings day.

Intuitions, She Said

Intuitions, she said,
A treasured art I will hold with care,
A timeless bond beyond compare.

Seven years ago, her hands did create;
Through strokes and hues, she read my soul,
As if we were bound by years untold.

The love I hold for this art so rare
Will never fade beyond words can speak—
An everlasting gift in brush and hues,
From a hijab beauty with skill on display.

Her hand, her heart, both spoke to me;
The piece of art she held, now mine to keep—
An eternal connection, perfectly made.

Echoes Of Nature

In my twenties, I first found my way
To this haven where I love to stay.
There, only nature's sound is heard—
The rustle of leaves, the song of birds,
The gentle whisper of the trees,
And the calming sigh of the evening breeze.

When night falls, a velvet shroud,
The stars above are a sparkling crowd.
In the jet-black night, fireflies lead my way,
Tales of the forest, timeless and bold.

In this place, my spirit roams free
Among the shadows of every tree—
A sanctuary from the world's demands,
Where time slips softly through my hands.

Every year, my heart leads me here
To the wild forest I hold close,
Where elephants roam with regal grandeur
In a land where I feel a timeless embrace.

Once chased by giants with tusks,
Yet never shattering my tranquil dream,
For this realm of ancient trees
My spirit finds its gentle ease.

Among the tigers, fierce and proud,
And gaurs that roam without a herd,
I walk with reverence, never in fear,
For I understand their purpose here.

They live in harmony, untamed and free,
In this place that holds deep mystery.
As long as I honor their sacred land,
In their presence, peace is found.

But gradually, change crept through the trees;
Encroachment spread like a silent disease.

Gone is the refuge from the city's din,
Where once I found peace deep within.
In the jungle's heart, my solace waved,
Leaving memories of what remained.

Yet still, I hold those moments close,
When the jungle sang and the night was clear.
In dreams, I wander through that space,
Searching for "Echoes of Nature."

A Life Reborn in Sobriety

Once rich with means, I spent with ease,
Lavish nights and carefree sprees.
For friends and travels, no expense was spared—
In a life of leisure, I was ensnared.

With each indulgence, I craved still more,
Ignoring the toll of an emptying store.
In alcohol's grip, I sought escape,
Chasing pleasure from dawn to dusk.

The more I spent, the less I gained;
My fortune shrank, yet I remained,
Blind to the truth that wealth can fade,
Lost in the shadows of choices made.

Until one day, I faced the truth—
An empty balance, a squandered youth.
I learned too late the cost of my ways,
In the echo of past lavish days.

My fortune flowed like a river's song;
In company of friends, I felt I belonged.
I shared my wealth with open hands,
In a world of indulgence and shifting sands.

Yet as my riches slipped away,
I reached for help in disarray.
Those I had treated well now out of sight,
Offered aid but spoke of their plight.

My body ached, my health declined;
With every drink, I felt confined.
Even love turned its back on me
When empty wallets were all to see.

In time, I saw this was not my fate—
To walk in shadows, isolate.
I could not stop quickly for fear of the fall,
So step by step, I answered the call.

Then came a morning bright and clear,
Awakening to a world sincere.
For the first time, without a drink,
I breathed in the air and felt the dawn light.

In nature's welcome, I found my way,
Renewed by hope with each new day.
The world around me fresh and free—
A life reborn in sobriety.

Faded Reveries Of Eighth Grade

In eighth grade, the days flew.
A new school under the city light.
I did not notice her in my first class,
A taller girl who sat in the back row.

But as the months began to glide,
I caught her smile, her eyes so rare.
A gray eye gleam, unique and beautiful,
And soon I found myself lost in her stare.

Roll call by the teacher and her response with a sweet voice,
With ease that made my heart grow fond.
A bet was made, which I can't remember what it was,
Yet losing brought a gift not so small.

A chocolate bar's pack, a symbol brief;
She took it, then gave it back in sweet belief.
Her manners spoke of something kind,
Which she accepted the gift in front of all.
I thought perhaps it was love I'd found,
But at thirteen years, such thoughts aren't sound.
Infatuation, just a spark,
A passing light in youth's brief dark.

A card I sent, unknown, unsigned,
With childish hope she'd know my mind.
But book post bore its tiny fine;
As soon she traced it back to me.

Her friends, they searched my bag for proof,
A secret game beneath the roof.
They found my script; the game was done,
And I, the 'Unknown Sender,' was the one.

Yet love was not our destined course in eighth grade;
The crush, it faded without force.
For school and life took hold that year
And left behind a memory so dear.

Ripples Of An Unknown Motif

In the silence of the morning light,
I found myself in solitude's hug.
A world once vivid now turns gray;
Without you here, it's an empty space.

The laughter fades like a distant dream;
The echoes of joy no longer sing.
A longing heart with a silent plea
For the warmth and love you used to bring.

The stars above seem dim and cold;
The moonlight casts a lonesome glow.
For without you, the nights are long,
And time moves with a heavy, aching flow.

Yet in my heart, I hold you near,
In every thought and whispered invocations,
Hoping for the day you return
To fill my life with the love we shared.

With Each Tug & Release I Ascend High Sky

I am a kite, colorful and valiant,
Crafted and shaped in rhombus, a spectacle to observe.
My tether stretched to the earth below,
In the pilot's hand, I glided with the breeze.

With each tug and release, I ascended high,
Yet the space persisted just beyond the blue sky.
My vibrant colors brought joy to all
While I drifted aloft, unaware of the steep fall.

But as the thread slackened, I climbed in hope,
While tightening lines pressed against my spine.
A worry deepened, a fear of despair—
Would my spine shatter under the pilot's pull?

Excitement and greed urged him to pull,
A fierce yank, and my spine felt the crack.
The pressure of wind tore through my skin—
No blood would flow, yet the pain was within.

Twisting and twirling, I spiraled down,
Uncertain of fortune, where I'd be bound.
Again and again, I twirled in the wind,
Till caught in a tree, I hung in unease.

Head down, I looked at the ground below,
Bound by fate beneath a watchful star.
In silence, I pondered the price of flight,
For the joy of the sky was swallowed by night.

A 23 Year Old Poised Woman

A young woman, twenty-three, poised in ease,

She strolled with one shoe adorned in white with turquoise lace.

As she waded through the downpour, her legs

Glimpsed first, glistening with lustrous beauty.

A purple dress that kissed her knees drew my gaze.

A yellow umbrella in her hand, bold by her side,

Yet wind and rain claimed half her path with pride.

The storm clutched at her, but she stood unbowed,

In half-wet vigor, moving along a winding road through the forest.

With a slow, deliberate pace, she passed,
And I wondered where she'd lost her shoe
And why not hold the other, walk side by side.
I watched her retreat, calm amidst the fall,
No rush, no balance, no care.

High steps hindered by her one-shoe foot,
Yet she still moved- no pause, no look.
What saga lies quietly in her gentle pace?
What secret dwells in her unhurried grace?

Her silhouette remains like art untold,
A story in my mind, a treasure of gold.
Yet the canvas white eludes my hand-
Her beauty is more than I can stand.
A friend I know, with brush and hues,
Could capture what I cannot outline.
A woman of art, both skilled and true,
Might bring to life what time cannot undo.

Waiting For Merlin

When I saw her first she was battling the grip of a cold,

Sneezed like a cat, dainty and neat, a quirky charm so sweet.

I was in a brewing session and my orbs followed her like a light.

She sneaked outside the cafe to sneeze, I looked her with desire,

A fascinating distraction in my caffeinated view.

I watch her beauty;

Yet she's fixed on cell phones back to back.

Her focus so keen, In a world of screens where her eyes belong.

I think she looked at me, but just once,

I wish to speak,but let the moment slip by.

A few days later we crossed paths in a Galleria

I smiled and asked " Have we seen before?"

"Yes" she replied with a grin.

We exchanged our names and whispered a soft goodbye,

Thus we met once more as fate called.

'Waiting for Merlin'; longing for our paths to cross again,

Where the Siren's brew and the whispers swing.

The Ticket Checker's Smile

I almost missed the train today,
The doors held open in their way.
Lucky timing, I climbed inside;
The train was lucky to have me ride.

Just then, I caught sight of a movie star's face,
Masked and hidden in her seat.
Moving on, a tall young woman caught my eyes,
A crew member, calm, standing by.

With bags stowed high, I found my seat,
Then noticed someone else to meet.
The ticket checker, a woman bold,
With a choppy bob and lips of deep wine cold.

I smoothed my hair, readied my grin,
As she approached to mark my fare.
She asked the man beside me first,
Then looked my way—I felt a burst.

I smiled with care,
Hoping she'd stay right there.
But soon she left and found a spot,
One seat away, where she forgot

And took a nap, her head at ease.
I wished to sit close by, our gazes to meet,
To share a smile and say "hello"
In that soft moment, warm and slow.

Sense Of Solace

In a world where shadows sometimes fall,
And words can wound or lift and stand,
We search for light,
A chance to give respect.

For some, the path is filled with fear,
Their voices lost—they cannot hear
The gentle call of kindness,
A whispered hope, a listening ear.

Yet still, beneath the surface,
A spark of mercy never dies;
It flickers in the darkest night,
A beacon warm, a guiding light.

So let us stand despite the storm,
With open hearts and spirits warm,
To build a bridge where rifts have grown,
And plant respect where seeds are sown.
For in the end, we're all the same—
A human soul, a fragile flame.

And with each act of gentle care,
We weave a world we all can share.
In a world where hearts can turn so cold,
And selfish minds take a firm stand,
I've given love, pure and true,
Yet still, the storms have broken through.

In moments small, they chose to run,
To cast their shadows in the light,
With overthought and needless strain,
They spread their clouds, bring forth the rain.

Yet in the quiet, I find my peace,
A gentle place where worries cease,
A space where whispers of the heart
Remind me of a brighter start.

So I choose the path of silence,
To hold my ground, to find my place,
Where joy is simple, talks are few,
Where I can be where skies are blue.

For in the stillness, I reclaim
The love I've given, just the same—
A steady light, a mild remedy,
A quiet heart that finds its calm.
This resonates with my feelings,
And offers a sense of solace.

The Black Hat, White She-Cat

An Oriental sweep of eyeliner,
A ponytail through the cap,
Jet Black second skin,
Black crossover straps, white soles.

Nude Wheat-Pink nails,
Her eyes hidden beneath the hat's obscure.
The Black Hat, White She-Cat,
A mystery draped in the shadow and matte.

Gate No. 13
Gate No. 13

I Am Raya, This Is My Electronic Mail

A book, a bookmark, the last page,

Ninety minutes to next flight.

Perfumes, time-wears and sunglasses,

I drifted from store to store.

Stopped to shop for distinctive scents,

Picked up the most woody and spicy oriental Pour Homme.

Browsing through sunglasses, exploring,

When suddenly, my eyes caught a cascade of voluminous curly hair.

She was attractive-plump and petite,

I stole a look back seeking her name, a trace online.

Longing to prolong our passing encounter,

Yet left with refusals and quiet goodbyes.

Walking towards Gate-13,

A sweet voice beckoned me to turn to listen-

A tender hand gesture, a spark of connection,

Held briefly in that transient moment.

A white miniature folded sheet,

With blue ink running in letters.

"I am Raya; this is my Electronic Mail."

Touching The Atmosphere, Igniting The Night

I gazed at the night sky,
Beneath the soft moonlight.
Tomorrow's whispers danced at the night,
Filling my thoughts with hope and light.

As I counted the stars, my thoughts turned to my friends,
The laughter we shared for the day, the joy in our way,
Will stay in my heart like the stars on display.

A golden flashlight in the sky caught my wandering eye,
Like a burning ember, it flickered so high.
In that quick moment, time seemed to freeze,
Even my blink paused in awe of the breeze.

I did not know what I had seen,
A comet's trial in the sky so unique.
A piece of space rock burning bright,
Touching the atmosphere, igniting the night.

A Cherished Hope, Like A Distant Star

I hold a dream, a wish unseen,
A hope that stays, yet serene.
Its future lies in shadows still,
Unknown if it will be fulfilled.

You might assume it as a common wish,
But for me, it's a lifetime bliss.
Not bound by place or transient thing,
For its presence in an endless spring.

It's a heartfelt plea
To share this moment with one who loves me through and through,
Holding hands at the cliff's gentle crest,
Watching the sunset as the horizon melts in hues of gold and pink.
To ride a bicycle down a quiet street,
With one who loves me through and through,
Having her take the seat on the bicycle's front frame.
Though its simple longing, it remains afar,
A cherished hope, like a distant star.

RAY-BAN
CAFE
BUBBLE
KNOT
MK

Fashionista

A-single shot Espresso in hand,

I ponder the words of Donna Ashworth.

From the untouched wisdom of page 13,

My eyes were captured by a Caucasian skin toned foot,

And cherry red hued toe nails.

The Birko Flor flats.

The Black Empire MK logo pants.

The purple bubble knot shirts.

The ever-rose gold analog time wear.

The yellow tint aviator sunglasses.

The fresh face and body skin,
The ruby hued lip shades,
The wet black curly hairs,
The smile was engaging.

I desired for a quick look of her eyes,

To commence with a smile and wish to conclude in bed.

I looked at her at evenly spaced intervals.

There she slurps the final gulp of coffee,

As she neared the glass portal,

I observed her reflection in the pane.

And I felt the bittersweet warmth of knowing I might not see that,

Fashionista Again.

Oh My Moon! Why Are You So Whimsically Grand?

The luminous circle with beauty spots,
In his radiant glow, the night's beauty we see.
His craters, like markings on a timeless face,
Showering a celestial light, peacefully free.

Yet he cannot illuminate all night,
Sometimes veiled by clouds or the shadowed fall of the blue planet.
He vanishes and returns back in days,
Still shining beyond where our sight fades.

He orchestrates the ocean's shifting trace,
Crafting tides that rise and fall in rhythmic dance.
At the seashore, we marvel at his grand display,
From rolling waves to the crescent's soft cascade.

With a charm both cheeky and spirited,
He winks with a glow that lights up the sky.
With a white light so witty, a glow unplanned,
Oh, my Moon, why are you so whimsically grand?

Ringlet Tresses, Ringlet Tresses

Ringlet tresses weave a spell,

In every glance I see and tell.

Thick and wild, their charms displayed,

In their curls, my heart arrayed.

Curly hairs has danced through time,

From first love to a friend sublime.

In each run-in, coils appear-

A thread of fate or choice sincere?

From parties, travel, to close friends,
Their ringlets weave a tale so clear.
Is it destiny or chance I find,
In every curls that warms my heart?

Perhaps it's fate that guides my way
To meet the curls that light my day.
Yet none have stayed, though reasons vary,
From solid grounds to excuses airy.

Only one remains though distant matters;
A transient meet is across the oceans.
In every curls, a trace of grace,
But only one keeps her place.

May be I should heed the signs
And not pursue the curls that shine.
For many are but passing clouds,
Their love as thin as moving shrouds.
In their clasp, true hearts are rare;
Their love is transient, like the rest-
Ringlet, tresses, ringlet tresses.

Song Of Flight

I wish to be like a bird in flight,
Soaring high through the endless sky,
Riding on winds, feeling so light,
With freedom's call, I wish to fly high.

To glide above the world below,
In the vast expanse where dreams reside,
To touch the clouds where cool breezes blow,
And drift on the currents, far and wide.
Then gently descend to Earth's warm shore,
To rest among trees and whispering streams,
Finding solace in nature's gentle serenity,
While living a life that's full of dreams.

To rise without burdens, light and free,
Without the chains of earthly obsessions,
To be the bird that I long to be,
In a dance of boundless expressions.

Once haunted by humans, the birds now soar,
As some have learned to respect them more.
Awakened minds now understand,
That birds too have life in this shared land.

Predators may still seek them in flight,
For nature's cycle is theirs by right.
The carnivores, driven by need
Play their part in the food chain's creed.

Yet we find peace in nature's way,
Where balance and harmony hold sway.
In the grand design, every life has a place,
In the ever-turning wheel of grace.

So let the birds sing their song of flight,
In skies that stretch from day to night.
For in the web of life, we see
A fabric woven in unity.

Textual Serenade Trace

The simplest way to bridge the gap,
Is through a digital tap.
From personal cheer to formal notes,
A text message brings someone or everyone near.

In every text a story flows,
A modest way to share and smile.
For in each texts short and long,
Through message beeps the world grows.

In the realm of texts, we send our ways.
In every message, styles blend and play.
Connecting hearts in every way.
In texts brief form, Meanings may stray.
Without the face, Intentions fray.

Be mindful of lines you send,
And let your heart in Textual Serenade Trace.

All Evidence Against Me Fabricated With Care

My lover caught me red-handed, the pop-ups sudden glow,

A notification glimpse setting our troubles to start.

I pleaded my case, said I'd done no wrong,

The message was casual, the content was harmless-

A message from my ex, reaching out for a re-approach.

Her wishes and requests I clearly ignored,

Yet my lover, in doubt, reached out once more

To clear the air—but my ex left a scar,

Seizing the chance to spin her fortune's wheel.

A stranger's name was enough for my lover to doubt,

My promises crumbled, though honest and loyal.

Was it trust—or was it something more she knew?

Now I stand as just a name in the fray,

Caught between two women, a game I can't play.

The blame I accepted, though I did not err,

All evidence against me, fabricated with care.

The Brazilian Starlight

A silent nod that echoes through the digital ether,

Some cloud illusions in the vast social media landscape.

Her eyebrows and nose captured my eyes,

Her half-moon smile cradling a solitary dimple—

A poetic dance in the symphony of her looks.

Similar photos of her weave, yet each look reveals new facets:

The matte and glossy cherry-red lip shades,

The chiseled cheeks, the long black hair, the sexy bralette,

The crimson teardrop ruby pendant nestled in her neck chain, glowing softly.

An emerald meadow,

A lavender dream,

A turquoise sea,

And a midnight whisper charm maiden adornment.

Our hearts clutched swiftly, and I valued her deeply.
Our words danced freely, exchanging cell numbers.
In the rise and fall of conversation,
She revealed her two children and untied vows.

She was the heart's anchor, a mother's devotion crowned—
Nurturing kin with loyal love, balancing duty and care as one.
This drew me deeper into her orbit,
Fascinated by her nature.
She stood as the third in a quartet of siblings,
A melody woven between the notes of the eldest and youngest.

Despite the barriers of language and country,
Our smiles conversed in the fluency of the heart,
A silent longing bridging our differences,
A tender echo of connection.

A quiet bond that transcended our disparities;
Across vast distances, our coffee date may
Span many moons, or fate may lead us on paths that never
Intersect.

We continue to converse without wavering in confidence.

In the quiet spaces between our words, we sense the echo of

Longing that would follow if either of us ceased

To text or call.

Even in video calls, hand gestures weave tales,

And greetings blossom like flowers,

Painting our mobile screens.

We've cultivated strength—a mutual care holding

Each other's challenges and triumphs with empathy.

Side by side, we await hopes for the best to unfold before us.

Eyes in eyes, we endure, awaiting the daybreak that follows night.

The Brazilian starlight in my sky—a friend, a crush.

Her spirit stays in the corner of my purple heart.

Two Beds And A Coffee Machine

Two beds rest side by side,
In a quiet room where dreams reside.
Each one a tale, yet to be told,
Of rest and comfort, warm and bold.

A coffee machine hums its tune,
Brewing warmth for the morning bloom.
Its rich aroma fills the air,
A morning ritual beyond compare.

In the early light, the day begins,
With coffee's kiss and morning grins.
Two beds await the end of the day,
Where dreams and comfort gently sway.

Together they weave a simple scene,
Of daily life and moments serene.
In this space where peace aligns,
Two beds and a coffee machine entwine.

№23

Tales From Seat Number 23

I met her by chance, a stranger at first,
but soon words found their way,
and "hello" grew into hours.
Chats that began in weeks
became talks filling every day.
Two strangers, now close,
wove in ways words fail to describe.
I never meant to be there each moment,
yet I found myself there—
my time freely hers.

The second meet-up was in her town,
but this time held more.
On her birthday, we met at Starbucks,
a place of familiar smiles,
then moved on to another café.
A birthday cake and a few tarts,
our voices filling four hours,
an unhurried exchange.
Now we share something beyond
what words can speak—close friends,
bound by trust, by time.

The next day she wished to come
to see me off once more,
but a busy schedule held her in place.
And here I am on this train,
seat 23, pen in hand,
leaving behind a piece of today—
a quiet echo of us.

In the Void of Her Absence

I bite my lips, and tears run deep,
For the love I hold, the secrets I keep.
What is my fault to feel her there,
In every breath, in each quiet stare?

If I could speak of my heart's reach,
I'd gather the stars within my speech.
What wrong have I done but loved her true,
Like waves that touch the shoreline blue?

The memories stay, shadows cast,
Of a love once bright but fading fast.
She slipped her hand from mine and turned,
Left me to wander where desert flowers burned.

Alone, adrift like Neptune's moon,
Lost in a space so wide, so soon.
No warmth remains, no spark to see,
In this vast, forsaken space for me.

If only I could rise to the Sun's fierce light,
And end this ache, this endless night.
Again, I bite my lips; my cries collide,
For the love I lost, the tears I hide.

Hello Yuliia

“Usually, my pen flows like a coffee spill on a Monday morning—unstoppable, messy, and fueled with passion. But today, it’s just a lonely ink stick, fantasizing about a better tomorrow”

www.ingramcontent.com/pod-product-compliance
Lightning Source LLC
LaVergne TN
LVHW091058150826
845673LV00002B/632

9798896323525